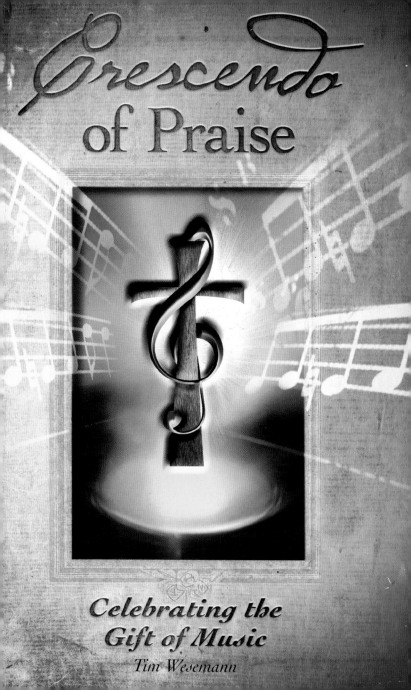

Crescendo of Praise

of Praise

Celebrating the Gift of Music

Tim Wesemann

www.CTAinc.com

Crescendo of Praise

Celebrating the Gift of Music
by Tim Wesemann
www.timwesemann.com

Copyright © 2006 CTA, Inc.
1625 Larkin Williams Rd.
Fenton, MO 63026-1205

ISBN 978-1-933234-03-8

Printed in Thailand

To _Nancy Dinsmore_

Grace . . .
Your Life Sings It!

Let the music of your praise,
which began when you
first heard
the heartbeat of your Savior,
never end.

From _Marilyn Altenbergen_

Date _July 12, 2007_

May our dependably steady
and warmly personal God
develop maturity in you
so that you get along with each other
as well as Jesus gets along with us all.
Then we'll be a choir—not our voices only,
but our very lives
singing in harmony
in a stunning anthem
to the God and Father of our Master Jesus!

Romans 15:5–6 *THE MESSAGE*

Crescendo of Praise

Table of Contents

Praise God, from whom all blessings flow;
Praise him, all creatures here below;
Praise him above, ye heav'nly host;
Praise Father, Son, and Holy Ghost.
Amen!

Thomas Ken, 1695

I truly desire that all Christians would love and regard as worthy the lovely gift of music, which is a precious, worthy, and costly treasure given to mankind by God. The riches of music are so excellent and so precious that words fail me whenever I attempt to discuss and describe them.

-6-

scendo
of Praise

. . . Next to the Word of God, the noble art
of music is the greatest treasure in the world.
It controls our thoughts, minds, hearts, and spirits.

. . . This precious gift has been given to man alone that he
might thereby remind himself that God has created man for
the express purpose of praising and extolling God.

Martin Luther
(1558; from his Foreword to Georg Rhau's Symphoniae iucundae)

A crescendo of voices in Heaven sang o

The kingdom of the world is now

Kingdom of our God and his Messi

He will rule forever and e

Revelation 11:15 THE MESS

Martin Luther penned words filled with power and with truth—see pages 6–7! Music *is* a precious, worthy, and costly treasure given by God! Discussing and describing the riches of music and its effect on our lives *can* indeed prove difficult—but definitely worth doing!

Whether you are a full-time or part-time musician or simply someone who appreciates music for the heavenly gift that it is, we pray the words in this book will bring you closer to God the Father, the Ultimate Director of all music, and to His Son, Jesus, who danced on the grave of death for us. May your life and mine—offer up a crescendo of praise to the one true God of the Bible. May he receive all thanks and glory for all he is and all we have become because of his love toward us in Jesus, our Savior.

Through the work of the Holy Spirit, this book, like the gift of music, is meant to

- invigorate faith;
- quiet troubled hearts;
- encourage personal music ministries;
- motivate new avenues of service;

- strengthen leaders;

- teach the riches of God's grace;

- tell stories of our Lord's goodness;

- touch emotions; and

- direct a crescendo of praise heavenward
  to the Creator of music!

e peaceful rests between measures, the praise-filled notes of
ipture and some encouraging quotes in harmony with them
bring you comfort and inspiration.

he back of this book you will find a journal—a keepsake—
vhich you can record your responses to a variety of questions
arding God's gift of music and his orchestration of your
ticipation in it as a part of your personal service to God's
ple. Fill it out! Then, perhaps years from now, you or your
ily can return to your words in moments of reflection to find
ouragement there!

you reflect on the treasure of music, may the Spirit of God
tinue to grow your faith, making your life more and more
escendo of praise to your Savior, Jesus Christ.

This is the day the LORD has made;
let us rejoice and be glad in it.

Psalm 118:24

In the beginning God created the heaven and the earth. G said, "Let there be light," and there was light. When he said, "Let there be an expanse in the midst of the waters," it was so God merely spoke the Word, and everything we know and se came into being. But when did God say, "Let there be music"

Do you know where the Bible first mentions music? The ans might surprise you. Genesis begins with the account of God's creation of the world, including Adam and Eve. The account of the first couple's fall into sin, the birth of Cain and Abel, and unfortunately, the first jealousy and murder, follow in quick succession.

Then the Bible notes the descendants of Cain. A few generati pass (within a few verses), and we find the names of Lamech and his wife, Adah, who gave birth to two sons:

> *[Jabel] was the father of those who dwell in tents and has livestock. His brother's name was Jubal; he was the father all those who play the lyre and pipe.*
>
> Genesis 4:20–21 ESV

bal—the maker of the first musical instruments. It isn't hard
guess where musical terms such as *jubilee* and *jubilate* find
ir origin.

om there on, music serves as a backdrop for the history of
d's people. Scripture describes, for instance, music played

- in worship;

- at the crowning of royalty;

- during marches into battles;

- in national triumphs;

- to soothe kings in anger or distress;

- at the offering of sacrifices;

- in joy;

- in mourning;

- in heaven; and

- as a symbol of judgment.

The Bible refers to teachers of music, choir directors, chief musicians, and temple chambers for musicians.

Biblical musicians used a noteworthy variety of instruments:

- Horns

- Cymbals

- Flutes

- Harps

- Lyres

- Pipes

- Tambourines

- Trumpets

- Zithers

, who played these instruments and sang the Bible's songs? ...eman, Asaph, Ethan, Jaaziel, Unni, Eliab, and Benaiah—to ...me only a few (1 Chronicles 15:16–29). The book of Psalms ...cords many of the words of these musicians, while 1 and ...Chronicles give us some great insight into the lives of the ...usicians appointed by the Levites at the request of King David ... service in God's house. As king, David commanded the ...iefs of the Levites to appoint singers who would also "play ...idly on musical instruments" in order to raise sounds of joy ...praise to God (1 Chronicles 15:16 ESV)!

*Music expresses
that which cannot be put into words
and that which cannot
remain silent.*

Victor Hugo

*Where words fail,
music speaks.*

Hans Christian Andersen

Let the peace of Christ rule in your hearts,
since as members of one body
you were called to peace.
And be thankful.
Let the word of Christ
dwell in you richly
as you teach and admonish one another
with all wisdom,
and as you sing psalms,
hymns and spiritual songs
with gratitude in your hearts to God.
And whatever you do,
whether in word or deed,
do it all in the name of the Lord Jesus,
giving thanks to God the Father through him.

Colossians 3:15–17

Historical Grace Note

t's switch keys for a moment, to take a brief look at who these evites" were and what they did. You may know that the Levites scended from the third of Jacob's twelve sons, Levi. When God ough Joshua divided the Promised Land of Canaan up between various clans descended from Jacob, the Levites did not eive a separate region as an inheritance from God. Instead, LORD himself was to be their inheritance. The Levites lived ide towns scattered across the entire land where they and their scendants were to serve as priests and overseers of Israel's rship life.

nique subset of Levites became priests. So although all priests re Levites, not all Levites were priests. They served at the ernacle from ages 30 to 50 but had other duties ore and after (Numbers 4:3, 23, 30).

Among other important tasks, Levites were responsible for the music that brought praise to God's name. In the last days of his reign, King David counted 38,000 Levites set aside for service. David divided them into several groups. For example, he set 4,00 aside to offer praises to the LORD with the instruments he had made for praise (1 Chronicles 23:1–6). By the time 1 Chronicles was written, the Levite families formed 24 guildlike associations characterized by the types of instruments they played.

Women joined with men in offering praise to the LORD, their Creator and Deliverer, throughout the Old Testament Scriptures. Groups of women sang and praised God with instruments to commemorate acts of God and triumph in battl For example, Miriam sang and led God's people in worship after the battle at the Red Sea (Exodus 15:20). Larger groups of women celebrated David's great victory over the giant Goliath (1 Samuel 18:6–7). Deborah commemorated the defeat of an oppressive heathen king by writing and singing a hymn of praise to the one true God (Judges 5:1–31).

e'd be remiss if we didn't mention the psalms again. What
important part they played in the musical history of Israel's
ople and in the worship of their God—and ours! Many of
 hymns and songs that were used in temple and personal
rship are found in the book of Psalms, and approximately
 f of the Psalms have superscriptions indicating the musical
 companiment customarily used with these encouraging hymns
hope.

us, from Genesis to Revelation, music finds its history and
ry purpose in the Bible. It's as if God said from the beginning,
et there be music, and may its sound be a constantly growing
escendo of praise to the glory of my name from the creation
d into all eternity!"

Sing, O Daughter of Zion;
shout aloud, O Israel!
Be glad and rejoice with all your heart,
O Daughter of Jerusalem!
The LORD has taken away your punishment,
he has turned back your enemy.
The LORD, the King of Israel, is with you;
never again will you fear any harm.
On that day they will say to Jerusalem,
"Do not fear, O Zion;
do not let your hands hang limp.
The LORD your God is with you,
he is mighty to save.
He will take great delight in you,
he will quiet you with his love,
he will rejoice over you with singing."

Zephaniah 3:14–17

Shout for joy to God, all the earth;
sing the glory of his name;
give to him glorious praise!

Psalm 66:1–2 ESV

Heavenly
Harmonies

The book of Revelation overflows with words of praise, songs, and music. The book that gives us a glimpse of heaven also lets us listen in on heaven's harmonies. The angels, elders, and multitudes sing and shout their praise to the Lamb of God sacrificed for the salvation of the world.

The Revelation of John tells of

- the four living creatures who never stop proclaiming their words of praise:

> *Holy, holy, holy*
> *is the Lord God Almighty,*
> *who was, and is, and is to come.*
> *Revelation 4:8*

- the conquerors, saints, redeemed by the Lamb and overwhelmed by his love, his sacrifice, singing the song of Moses and the song of the Lamb:

> *Great and amazing are your deeds,*
> *O Lord God the Almighty!*
> *Just and true are your ways,*
> *O King of the nations!*

> *. . . For you alone are holy.*
> *All nations will come*
> *and worship you,*
> *for your righteous acts*
> *have been revealed.*
> Revelation 15:3–4 ESV

• the roar, as of a great multitude in heaven, shouting:

> *Hallelujah!*
> *Salvation and glory and power*
> *belong to our God.*
> Revelation 19:1

d the praises of heaven continue across page after page, npse after glimpse of our future, a future filled with praise, h song, with shouts of victory.

will, no doubt, count the privilege of singing praises to our ior among the greatest joys of our inheritance in the mised Land of heaven. But what about now?

uld it amaze you to know that right now, even as you read se words, the Lord himself rejoices over you with singing?

Yes, the Lord himself sings over us! God, through the prophe reminds us of this fact in Zephaniah 3:17. The Lord encourag us to find our hope in him. Even in our darkest times, he quie us with his love and rejoices over us.

If the Lord sang over his Old Testament people, then he certainly continues to sing over each of us today! It's almost unimaginable, but we have God's word on it. Heaven's harmonies surround us. No, there's nothing we've done to deserve it. Our good works don't make him sing in joy. The rhythms of our lives are often offbeat and out of sync with his direction. We sing our melodies off-key and out of tune with heaven's harmony of love, of joy, and of peace.

Still, Scripture assures us that Christ Jesus has won for us a place in heaven's choir nonetheless. His robe of righteousness won on his own bloody cross—covers us. Our sins are gone, and now Jesus brings us to the Father, who rejoices over us with singing!

What a blessed truth! Even as we make music that honors Go the Lord of the universe gracefully rejoices over us with singi Talk about inspired music! Imagine it if you can. Rejoice in that truth and let the crescendo of your praise grow stronger and stronger!

Behold, God is my salvation;
I will trust, and will not be afraid;
for the LORD GOD is
my strength and my song,
and he has become my salvation.

Isaiah 12:2 ESV

May our Lord Jesus Christ himself
and God our Father, who loved us and by his grace gave us
ernal encouragement and good hope, encourage your hearts
and strengthen you in every good deed and word.

2 Thessalonians 2:16–17

Praise him! Praise him!
Jesus, our blessed Redeemer!
Sing, O Earth,
His wonderful love proclaim!
Hail him! Hail him!
Highest archangels in glory;
Strength and honor
give to his holy Name!
Like a shepherd,
Jesus will guard his children,
In his arms he carries them all day long:
Praise him! Praise him!
Tell of his excellent greatness;
Praise him! Praise him!
Ever in joyful song!

Fanny J. Crosby

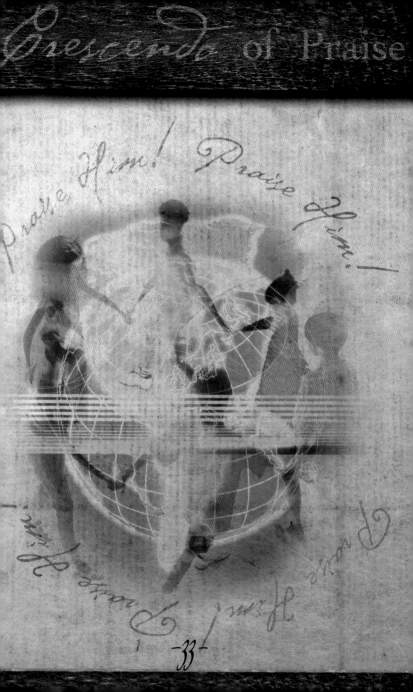

*Throw yourselves into the work of the
Master, confident that nothing you do for
him is a waste of time or effort.*

1 Corinthians 15:58 THE MESSAGE

When God called Isaiah into heaven's service, heaven's music surrounded the new prophet. Angels soared around him as they called to one another:

> *Holy, holy, holy is the LORD Almighty;*
> *the whole earth is full of his glory.*
>
> *Isaiah 6:3*

The word *holy* means "set apart." The angels used the word in triplicate to emphasize that the LORD in his glory is set apart like no one else.

Do you regard your calling, as one who offers God a crescendo of praise, holy? We know that God has called us as his people out of the world system around us to live as part of his holy nation (1 Peter 2:9). We are holy in Christ's holiness.

Our God has also placed a variety of other holy callings on our lives. Musician. Employee. Friend. Parent. Spouse. Employer. Child. Student. . . . Did I mention *musician?*

ile you live your life as a continuous crescendo of praise to
d, he blesses you with important and unique musical gifts,
well as opportunities to use those gifts to his glory and the
lding up of the body of Christ. He calls you joyfully to
ve him with the precious gift of music.

you receive that calling, angels surround you, just as they
rounded Isaiah. They shout out their praise to our holy God,
ing you to join them in praising, honoring, and thanking
through music, as well as with everything else you do.
you hear them?

> *Holy, holy, holy is the LORD Almighty;*
> *the whole earth is full of his glory.*
>
> *Isaiah 6:3*

Do these lyrics pull at your heartstrings? Does your spirit pulse with excitement, in turn, as you consider the words of the calling?

King David commanded the chiefs of the Levites to appoint their brothers as singers and instrumentalists and set them to the task of raising sounds of joy to the Lord! What a tremendous calling—to raise sounds of joy to the LORD! Don't just stand in awe looking back at this historical event. Instead, join them! Raise your own sounds of joy to the Lord today! Look in the mirror and recognize that God has singled you out, given you precious gifts with which to serve him. You have been called by God to raise sounds of joy heavenward! What an honor! What a calling! What a gracious Giver of Gifts our God is!

He has created . . .

- some to lead musicians and others to follow musical notes;

- some to ring bells and others to play music that rings a bell in people's minds;

- some to teach music and others to teach those who teach music;

- some to sing in harmony and others to help musicians live in harmony;

- some to play in an orchestra and others to orchestrate a community concert;

- some to hum hymns and others to keep hymns from becoming ho-hum;

- some to play the strings and others to pull strings to fund the music program;

- some to tune instruments and others to stay in tune with the latest instruments;

- some to construct instruments and others to offer
  instrumentalists constructive criticism;

- some to work sound boards and others who never
  get bored no matter the sounds of praise;

- some to sing on key with the notes on the black and white
  keys of a piano and others to sing praises on the notes
  that are between the black and white keys; and

- some to work behind the scenes and others to be seen
  daily praising the Lord through music!

many gifts! So many opportunities! So many people called to
ise God and lift up his people through the gift of music!
many! So many!

So many prayers are needed for those on whose lives God has placed a musical calling. Let's join our hearts in prayer and regularly offer up to God's throne of grace petitions for . . .

- directors of music ministries;
- choir members;
- instrumentalists;
- bodies of believers in need of music leaders or accompanis
- choirs or bands struggling for whatever reason;
- children's choirs;
- soloists;
- prayer partners for those called to minister through mus
- music programs in need of financial support;
- musicians not using their gifts to God's glory;
- people listening to and otherwise involved in the gift of music — that the Holy Spirit would grow their faith;
- music ministries throughout the world;
- music teachers;
- music schools;

- music camps;

- individuals teaching music lessons; and

- music therapists and others who use music to help those with special needs.

[Li]sten! God is calling! Calling you to praise, worship, and thank [Hi]m through music. Calling you to pray for music ministries and [to s]upport other musicians offering their gifts for God's glory. [M]ost important, he is calling you through the Holy Spirit to live [as] his forgiven, saved, and dearly loved child of God . . . and [tha]t is what you are and always will be! (1 John 3:1).

[Li]sten! God is calling!

May the words of my mouth and the meditation of my heart
be pleasing in your sight, O LORD,
my Rock and my Redeemer.

Psalm 19:14

Rejoice, O pilgrim throng!
Rejoice, give thanks, and sing;
Your festal banner wave on high,
The cross of Christ your king.
Rejoice! Rejoice!
Rejoice, give thanks, and sing!

With voice as full and strong
As ocean's surging praise,
Send forth the sturdy hymns of old,
The psalms of ancient days.
Rejoice! Rejoice!
Rejoice, give thanks, and sing!

44

With all the angel choirs,
With all the saints on earth
Pour out the strains of joy and bliss,
True rapture, noblest mirth.
Rejoice! Rejoice!
Rejoice, give thanks, and sing!

Praise him who reigns on high,
The Lord whom we adore:
The Father, Son, and Holy Ghost,
One God forevermore.
Rejoice! Rejoice!
Rejoice, give thanks, and sing!

Edward H. Plumptre (1821–91)

May the words of my mouth and the meditation of my heart
be pleasing in your sight, O LORD,
my Rock and my Redeemer.

Psalm 19:

Tessitura. In case you don't recognize that musical term, let me explain that it refers to the range of an instrumental part or the vocalist's parts in a composition.

The notes on any given musical score can take a musician from great heights to deep, low tones. Instruments and human voices alike have limited range. Sopranos aren't going to hit the notes a bass vocalist is accustomed to singing. A piccolo and a sousaphone share little in either appearance or musical range.

Stepping outside the musical score to look at the composition our life's symphony, we note our own personal, limited tessitura. We don't know everything. We can't do everything. Our strength has definite boundaries, and we push beyond them at our own peril. Some days our worst problems grow out of the fact we don't know what we don't know! It's more than a cliché no one is perfect. Though given an opportunity, many of us still would try living solo lives, lives unbounded by our God's commands and lived for our own pleasures and for the world's acclaim.

And, as if that weren't enough, our lives are filled with *glissando*. Perhaps you recognize the term. It refers to sliding between the notes. We not only try to live as if we had no limits and as if we could get along quite well living solo lives apart from our Savior,

also find ourselves too often sliding between God's
wavering notes of faithfulness and our notes of unfaithfulness.
slide between this note and that note, hoping to satisfy our
n desires. We seek out melodies to tickle our itching ears,
lodies that clash, melodies out of harmony with God's voice.

, we slide from one note to another. Yes, our range is limited
e intend to live our lives as a solo performance.

just then, when all hope seems lost, Jesus Christ —
Composer, The Maestro, The Director of all Directors — steps onto
stage. Suddenly our range becomes limitless. Every note
now become a note of praise, a note adding to all creation's

continuing crescendo of praise! The limit of tessitura disappea
during duets we sing with our Savior! Nothing limits what we
can do with Christ as our partner. Nothing limits the praise w
can offer, the service we can raise. With Jesus taking the role
Concertmaster in our lives, our joy and peace blend in perfect
harmony with the Prince of Peace!

But turn the page and you'll discover the piece you're playing
has been arranged for many more parts. The Conductor lifts I
baton and signals for a full choir and its orchestra to join in as
the praise increases in volume! Your brothers and sisters in
faith, the saints of all time and every place, join in the chorus.
All lift songs of thanksgiving and praise heavenward. The mus
is not only spirited, it is Spirit-filled, as the Spirit of God mov
through it by his Word to change lives in eternal ways:

- The Holy Spirit creates faith through God's Word—
  whether spoken, read, or sung!

- The Holy Spirit blesses those who recognize and give
  God glory in all they do, including using their
  musical gifts!

- The Holy Spirit causes God's people to respond to the
  love, forgiveness, and salvation of Jesus Christ by lovi

forgiving, and touching hearts and lives around them with the Savior's joy and peace.

- The Holy Spirit keeps us growing in faith, which means the crescendo of praise continues to grow through all our days!

d's Spirit lives within us and leads our souls to sing and play ful music of praise throughout our lives!

———◦(((◦)))◦———

ne, Holy Spirit, stir up the music of heaven within us! Cause our days e filled with music that gives God the glory and praise his holy name rves! Amen.

———◦(((◦)))◦———

riend once asked the great composer Haydn why his church music was always so full of gladness. He answered,

"I cannot make it otherwise. I write according to the thoughts I feel. When I think upon my God, my heart is so full of joy that the notes ce and leap from my pen; and since God has given me a cheerful heart, it will be pardoned me that I serve Him with a cheerful spirit."

Henry Van Dyke

Take my life and let it be
Consecrated, Lord, to thee;
Take my moments and my days,
Let them flow in ceaseless praise;
Let them flow in ceaseless praise.

Take my voice and let me sing
Ever, only, for my King.
Take my lips and let them be
Filled with messages from thee;
Filled with messages from thee.

Take my love, my Lord, I pour
At thy feet my treasure store;
Take myself and I will be
Ever, only, all for thee.
Ever, only, all for thee.

Frances R. Havergal

Let every living, breathing creature praise GOD! Hallelujah!

Psalm 150:6 THE MESSAGE

The Unfinished Symphony of Praise

hat could be more poignant than an unfinished symphor
A great composer has heard magnificent music in his heart, an
he writes down the notes so others can share the music . . . on
to have something interfere, intervene. And the music is lost,
lost forever!

Psalm 137 falls into that category. The author writes these
words while living away from home. He and the rest of the
inhabitants of Judah have been overtaken by the Babylonians
and exiled to a foreign land. Their Jerusalem homes and land
have been plundered and raped, their temple destroyed. Famil
and friends lie gravely injured or even dead. And God's people
now live in captivity with heavy hearts and no joy to spur them
to praise.

By the rivers of Babylon we sat and wept
when we remembered Zion.
There on the poplars we hung our harps,
for there our captors asked us for songs,
our tormentors demanded songs of joy;
they said, "Sing us one of the songs of Zion!"

> *How can we sing the songs of the LORD*
> *while in a foreign land?*
> *If I forget you, O Jerusalem,*
> *may my right hand forget its skill.*

Psalm 137:1–5

...at a visual! The Babylonians insist the musicians play a song
...oy, but the harpists sit on the riverbanks, crying their eyes
...in response to what has happened to them and their
...eland. They have hung their instruments on the branches
...villow trees. Will they ever play again? It seems doubtful
...the future, bleak.

...listen! Do you hear it ever so softly in the distance? It is
...sound of a harp! It is the voice of a musician singing a song
...omfort, hope, and even joy! It is the song of the prophets
...od bringing good news to drown out the
...mentors' sarcastic demands!

The deep, rich voice of Isaiah sings:

> *Comfort, comfort my people, says your God.*
> *Speak tenderly to Jerusalem, and proclaim to her*
> *that her hard service has been completed,*
> *that her sin has been paid for,*
> *that she has received from the LORD's hand double*
> *for all her sins.*

Isaiah 40:1–2

Can you relate to the harpless, hapless people of God living in captivity? No doubt you can! Not because you're the "suffering musician" caricatured by the popular press, but because you live in a world filled with sin. With that sin come suffering, problems, and even death. Satan loves nothing more than to bring events and emotions into our lives intended to silence our song and persuade us to hang up our praise. Have you been there? Or are you there now?

- Perhaps you've allowed yourself to be held captive by addictive sin, and it's hard to offer songs of praise when guilt hangs heavy around your heart.

- Maybe you've been chosen for the solo, but your heart is heavy trying to break through the loneliness of living solo.

- Perhaps you stand on the risers as your choir practices for a joyful Christmas concert while your mind is hanging its hope on a year-end bonus to cover the costs of your overextended holiday credit line.

- Or maybe you wonder if the words of the Easter music you sing can bring any hope while you grieve the loss of a loved one.

atever situation has brought you to sit under a harp-filled , don't allow your hurts to drown out the music of another is nearby. He will finish the as-yet-unfinished symphony of r life. Like Isaiah, he sings a song of comfort and hope. He s, hanging from a tree down the road. The words of his song of forgiveness, love, and eternal life. His music soothes

troubled minds and hearts. The song he sings gives praise to h
Father in heaven while pulling you into the refrain extolling th
glory of God.

Soon you find yourself joining the chorus of those who love th
God-man who once hung in agony on a hill outside Jerusalem
so you need never hang up your harp or walk in despair away
from the harmonies of heaven. He has chosen you to take a pa
in the *Unfinished Symphony of Praise!*

One day, in heaven, this symphony will find its perfection . . .
but it won't end there. There is no end to the *Unfinished
Symphony of Praise* that began when the Holy Spirit created fai
within you and brought you to the cross to hear Jesus sing ou
"It is finished!"

Here on earth, many of God's people often find ourselves
wanting to "hang it up," and sometimes we want to hang up
more than our harps. We live in a world of sin. But we also li
in a world in which the Word became flesh and made his
dwelling among us. And he, Jesus Christ, is the ultimate
director of songs of joy. Into everything he orchestrates, he
masterfully writes rests for the singers and those playing

...truments of praise. He finds ways to surround us with fellow
...rist-following musicians to support us, to pick up our slack in
...es of weakness, and to play or sing in harmony with his
...rds of promise, hope, and help.

...you feel the praise for God's life and orchestration beginning
...build within you? Is the Spirit of God bringing you to a
...ater appreciation of the measure of his saving love for you?
...e you ready to grab your harp from the tree and join in the
...g of praise? The piece is titled *The Unfinished Symphony of*
...ise. Take your place. Grab your instrument—*be* God's
...trument!

...d let the crescendo of praise continue . . . without end!

Praise the LORD!
Praise God in his sanctuary;
praise him in his mighty heavens!
Praise him for his mighty deeds;
praise him according to his
excellent greatness!
Praise him with trumpet sound;
praise him with lute and harp!
Praise him with tambourine and dance;
praise him with strings and pipe!
Praise him with sounding cymbals;
praise him with loud clashing cymbals!
Let everything that has breath praise the LORD!
Praise the LORD!

Psalm 150 ESV

My heart is steadfast, O G
I will sing and make me
with all my be

Psalm 10

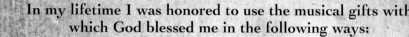

In my lifetime I was honored to use the musical gifts with which God blessed me in the following ways:

_____

_____

_____

_____

_____

_____

As of today, some of my favorite hymns are

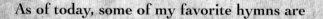

_____

_____

_____

_____

_____

_____

of today, some of my favorite praise songs/choruses are

_____

_____

_____

_____

_____

ave played the following instrument(s) at some point
my life:

_____

_____

_____

_____

_____

_____

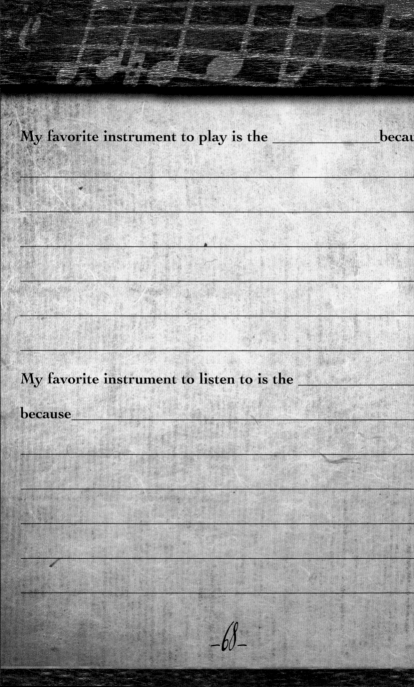

My favorite instrument to play is the _____becau

_____

_____

_____

_____

_____

_____

My favorite instrument to listen to is the _____

because_____

_____

_____

_____

_____

_____

ew of my favorite Christian musicians are

_____

_____

_____

_____

ew of my favorite secular musicians are

_____

_____

_____

e first memory I have of music is _____

_____

_____

_____

_____

When I was a little child, my favorite song was probably

_____

_____

_____

_____

_____

_____

God used the following people to bring me to have an

appreciation of his gift of music: _____

_____

_____

_____

_____

_____

Special prayers I want to offer, thanking God for his gift of music and musicians while asking for his help to use his gift as a continuous crescendo of praise in my life:

_____

_____

_____

_____

_____

_____

_____

_____

_____

_____

...d has used music in my life to shape me spiritually,
...cting my life and faith in the following ways:

...e: _____

_____

...e: _____

_____

...e: _____

_____

...ossible, I'd like the following music played at my funeral
...e day: _____

_____

_____

_____

_____